THE 100 BEST
CHILDREN'S ROOMS

BETA-PLUS

THE 100 BEST
CHILDREN'S ROOMS

CONTENTS

A real metamorphosis 6

A children's paradise in a contemporary seaside villa 10

In the attic 14

A passion for antiques 16

A spirit of freshness 18

Western inspiration. 20

Contemporary country style 24

Luxury and well-being 26

The rooms of Albane and Pierre 28

A girl's suite 30

An explosion of bright colours 32

Under the old beams. 34

Sober, warm and timeless 36

La Source 38

The rooms of Victor and Cato 42

A respectful renovation. 44

A contemporary space for Max and Ben 46

A warm and timeless aura 50

A perfect symbiosis. 54

A wonderful place to live 60

Peace and serenity 62

Functional yet warm and intimate 64

Picturesque. 66

Different accents. 68

A holiday home near the beach. 70

A true holiday feel 72

Surrounded by nature. 74

Young and contemporary 76

Paradise in pink 78

Anno 1642 80

The contemporary renovation of a former hunting lodge .82

A blend of timeless and contemporary: a balanced philosophy for living. 84

The complete transformation of a Belle Epoque country house 86

Living in a restored farmhouse 88

A romantic girl's room 90

Cosy minimalism 94

Peace and quiet 96

A lakeside residence near Geneva 98

Anglo-Saxon inspiration. 100

A chic home in a classic Georgian residence 104

Holiday feeling in Gstaad 106

The children's rooms of two mountain chalets. 108

An orange and white colour explosion. 112

Two children's rooms in London. 114

Cosy and intimate. 116

The bright children's rooms of Casa Nero 118

Loft story. 120

Cosmopolitan feeling 122

Baby & co : a paradise for (future) parents. 124

A perfect balance between classic and modern 134

Playful details. 136

Cosy home in solid wood 138

Perfect harmony 142

A warm and contemporary Rectory-style house 144

Warm feel in an austere design 146

Contemporary and timeless 148

Streamlined, classic and chic 150

The children's rooms of a historic notary's house 152

Maritime feel 154

Light and space in a seaside apartment 156

Extra depth 158

A refuge for the children. 160

Long Island style 162

Happy colours 164

Bright green and pastel. 166

Sense of space and calm 168

Endless views 170

A suite for the daughter 174

A true charming home 176

A real family home. 182

Full of character. 184

Space and light in a contemporary country house. 190

The attractions of an ancient farmhouse. 196

Inspired by the English countryside 198

A passion for beauty. 200

A passion for wood. 206

Paradise for a little princess 210

Poetry in colours. 212

Castle living 214

At home 216

An attractive style. 222

Long Island inspiration. 226

A colourful paradise. 230

A REAL METAMORPHOSIS

A rustic villa with a lot of oak and dark materials was transformed by Peter Ivens (interior and architecture agency Astra Loves Living) into a modern country residence: the residence experienced a true metamorphosis through a few strong interventions.

www.astralovesliving.com

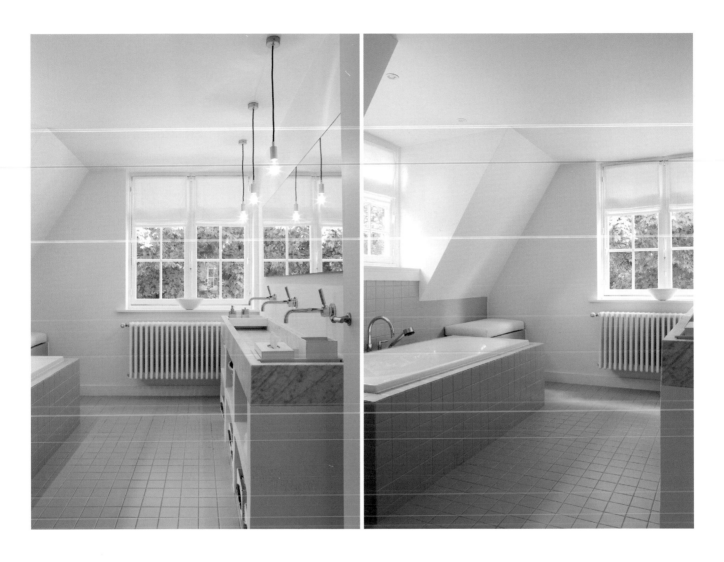

The first floor was furnished entirely for the children.
A bathroom with elongated hand basin in Carrara marble.

A CHILDREN'S PARADISE
IN A CONTEMPORARY SEASIDE VILLA

Interior architect Marie-France Stadsbader transformed two semi-detached
houses on the coast into a cosy weekend home for a young family.
Despite the limited surface each function was still given its space.
The top floor with the children's rooms is monochrome white: all the spaces are
designed in the same way to form a single whole. White walls combined with a
white painted parquet and fun objects ensure a pleasant living environment.
A real paradise for the children...

mst@cantillana.com

IN THE ATTIC

An enclosed convent farm built in the seventeenth century was
carefully restored by architect Bernard De Clerck.
The children's rooms are in the attic: intimate and full of atmosphere.

info@bernarddeclerck.be

The pink and blue bedrooms.

A PASSION FOR ANTIQUES

When the couple of antiques dealers Brigitte and Alain Garnier decided to restore the historic
Vaucelleshof (an abbey and farmhouse including 17th, 18th and 19th century buildings)
and make it their new home, they didn't forget the importance of the children's rooms.
The entire second floor is now reserved for the daughter and son of the house...

www.garnier.be

The girls' room.
The bed is covered with Ralph Lauren fabrics. A wine table on the left, old farmer's furniture from Drente on the right.

↖
The boy's room. A Swedish chest of drawers between the two beds.

→
A Canadian Adirondacks rocking chair beside a moose head and wooden interior shutters. An antique pine cheeseboard floor.

A SPIRIT OF FRESHNESS

This house covered with cedar shingles was created by AID Architects.
The lakeside surroundings inspired them for the design of the interior.
The house consists of several guest rooms, all conceived in the spirit of freshness,
without unnecessary details and with a preference for natural materials.

www.aidarchitecten.be

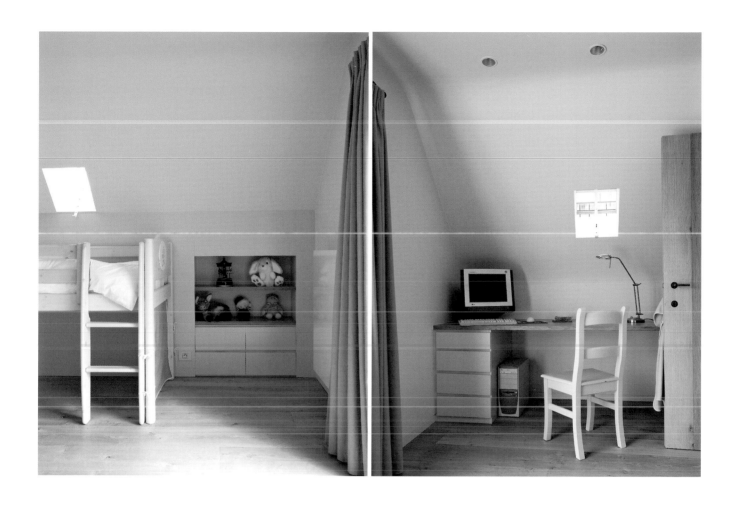

WESTERN INSPIRATION

The attic of an existing dwelling was revamped by Cy Peys /
Partners into a room with character and personality that serves as
a bedroom and a playing space for the elder son of the owner.
The ludic character and boy's style are accentuated by Western themes.

www.cypeys.com

The walls are clad in pine wood panels with a paint that leaves an apparent wood grain. The tinted floor is also in pine wood. Provided with tailor-made comfortable cushions, the play area is arranged underneath the slope of the roof to allow for a clear space at the center of the room. Functional drawers are discreetly incorporated under the play area.

The office table extends throughout the whole length of the area. Chairs are from Habitat.

↖
A spare bed is hidden in the drawer underneath the single bed.

View in perspective from the play area towards the bedroom. The wall cupboards that flank the play zone and the rest zone are made-to-measure. They reinforce the space and cohesion of this attic. The cupboards are in vertical strips of timber planks, contrasting the horizontality of the wall that helps to enlarge the room visually.

CONTEMPORARY COUNTRY STYLE

Architect Stany Dietvors has created balanced proportions
and volumes in a contemporary country house.
The flow between the different spaces is well constructed: the recently
renovated leisure room and the bedrooms demonstrate this idea.

The transition between the leisure room and the bedroom.

Happy and romantic prints provide a contemporary ambience.

↖
The leisure room was
created by Brussels interior
designer Nicolas Dervichian.
Furniture and cabinets by
Borja Veciana.

LUXURY AND WELL-BEING

The work of architecture and interior design company Themenos
has luxury and well-being as one of its leidmotivs.
Themenos' rooms, even those for the children, remain intimate and
personal spaces in harmony with the rest of the house.

www.themenos.be

Sleeping, playing and studying ... all in one big space.
The horizontal lines of the planed oak rejuvenate the whole.

THE ROOMS OF ALBANE AND PIERRE

Albane (4 years) and Pierre (5 and a half years) are the
children of interior designer Stéphanie Parein.
The small family lives in a house full of character nearby Brussels.

A GIRL'S SUITE

In this stately country house dating from 1914 and renovated by Q&M (Walter Quirynen),
the daughter has a real girl's suite: a spacious bedroom with a bathroom and shower.

walter.quirynen@skynet.be

This girl's bathroom (built by B&I) has a holiday atmosphere. with pebbles in the shower.

↖
The girl's bedroom with an
open gas fire. The marble
mantelpiece has been
retained. The oak parquet
upstairs is newly laid, but
has a timeless look.

AN EXPLOSION OF BRIGHT COLOURS

This resolutely New England-style manor house, transformed
by A.R.P.E. (Antoine de Radiguès) and the general construction
firm Macors, has been decorated by Lionel Jadot.
The boy's and girl's bedroom are a real explosion of
bright colours and teenager's fantasies...

lioneljadot@yahoo.fr   www.macors.be

The teenager's bedroom. The
explosion of bright colours is
dominated by rose and orange.
To please the young lady who
sleeps in this room, Mondrian's
work, which has been slightly
revised and updated, is on view.

UNDER THE OLD BEAMS

Sphere Concepts took care of the renovation of this listed farmhouse constructed at the beginning of the last century, and situated on an estate of thirty hectares. The complete interior design, including the materials and colours, was proposed and developed by Sphere in consultation with the owner. The old outbuildings and the house have new functions. The first floor contains the children's rooms: bedrooms, study and bathroom.

www.sphereconcepts.be

SOBER, WARM AND TIMELESS

In this report, Daskal-Laperre Interior Architects present the children's rooms of a renovated house for a family with young children. Their aim was to create a sober, warm and timeless home.

www.daskal-laperre.com

The children's bedrooms with their own bathroom in green glass
mosaic with a large bath and separate shower.

LA SOURCE

"La Source" is a sixteenth century stately home set in the Gascogne region and whose farm buildings have recently been fully renovated by interior designer Sarah Lavoine. Everything still had to be done: recovering the old stones from the outer walls, restructuring the garden, redrawing the boundaries of the rooms, building a swimming pool, and so on, and for once Sarah Lavoine herself was the customer. As soon as she acquired this domain, Sarah Lavoine knew exactly what it was she wanted: a large family home full of friends, with many living areas and large, very comfortable rooms for everyone. Sarah Lavoine modernised her house and at the same time gave it a warmer atmosphere. It was an enormous project and there is still a lot of work to be done, but the advantage of a holiday residence is that you can take all the time you need. Each room is named after the colour of the parquet (red, green, blue, etc.). In this report, Sarah Lavoine presents the children's rooms.

www.sarahlavoine.com

The red room with its large black iron arch and Bruder carpets on the red parquet.
The children's rooms are in blue and cherry red, each reflecting the colours of the bathrooms.

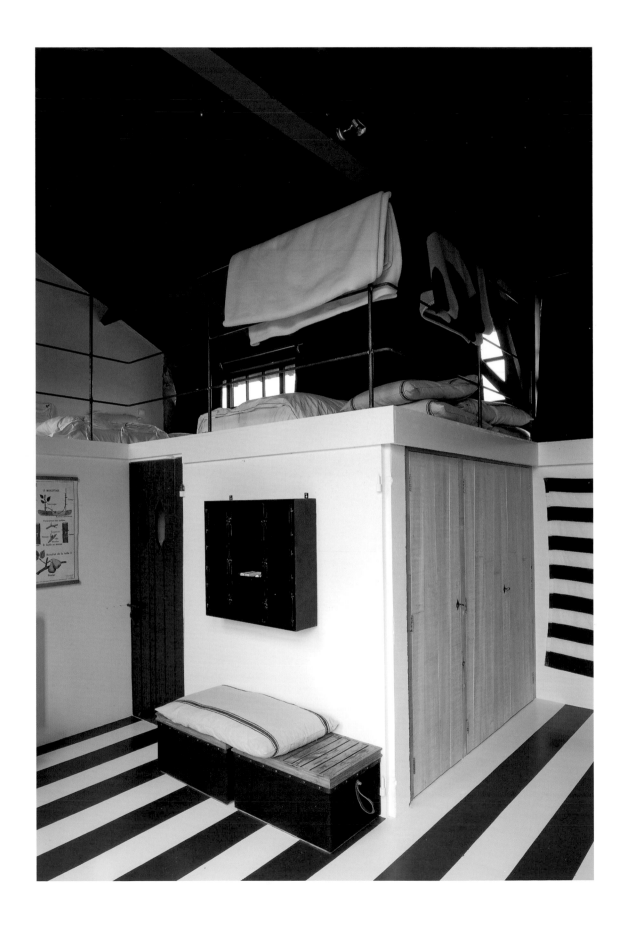

The henhouse interior, the children's domain. Sarah Lavoine painted the floor here in red and white to imbue the whole place with character and charm. The door panels were left natural.
The visible trusses were painted black. A shower room in black slate.

THE ROOMS OF VICTOR AND CATO

Paul Vanrunxt and Ludo Bruggen met each other almost twenty years ago.
One was passionate about architecture, the other one about new building
techniques and interior design. "Vincent Bruggen" became a
fact. Shortly after this the first show country house was built.
For the design of his own house, Paul Vanrunxt was inspired by
old mansions with high ceilings: a symbiosis of authenticity, timelessness and
temporary comfort - in the whole house, including both children's rooms.

www.vincentbruggen.be

A RESPECTFUL RENOVATION

This house has been carefully renovated by Costermans Villa Projects with respect for the distinctive original architecture and the valuable materials that were very much worth preserving.

www.costermans-projecten.be

This hobby room can be easily transformed into a guestroom due to the modular placing of the seat.

A CONTEMPORARY SPACE FOR MAX AND BEN

In a spacious country house constructed in Canadian wood skeleton, Vincent Bruggen
created a contemporary bedroom for the children of the house, Max and Ben.

www.vincentbruggen.be

A WARM AND TIMELESS AURA

Christel De Vos (RR Interior Concepts) created the interior
of this house built by Vlassak-Verhulst.
The children's rooms have the same warm and timeless aura of the rest of the house.

www.rrinterieur.be

A PERFECT SYMBIOSIS

In this recent Mi Casa project, the company, specialized in massive wooden construction, shows that the combination with a classical brick construction can equally lead to a perfect symbiosis. This country house, situated near the coast of Knokke, has been designed by the Bureau of Architects E&L Projects. Both outside as well as inside the use of massive wood brings in an extra dimension: a remarkable intimate and warm living environment which provides a permanent holiday feel.

www.micasa.be

The painted horizontal planking in two colours provides a fresh wainscoting.

In a Mi Casa house every inner wall is built and finished off with massive wooden planking: it suffices to choose your own color, and every room immediately gets a personal, warm touch.

A WONDERFUL PLACE TO LIVE

A family with two small children bought a dilapidated house in the countryside, designed
by a Brussels architect around 1930 in a modernist style inspired by Le Corbusier.
Stephanie Laporte created the interior design of the renovated house. The look is sober,
comfortable and functional, also in the children's rooms: a wonderful place to live.

www.stephanielaporte.be

The children's bathroom with an illuminated ceiling. Floors and walls in grey tiles. Surface with built-in washbasin in Corian.

↖
The children's bedroom with
a light-tinted parquet floor.

PEACE AND SERENITY

This metropolitan duplex apartment offers magnificent views and optimum incidence of light. To create a feeling of intimacy, the larger rooms were divided into different areas while retaining the loft concept by not using fixed walls. Although Nathalie Van Reeth selected different materials, she used the same tonality to preserve the loft's atmosphere so that the different areas blend together; a whole picture that radiates peace and serenity.

nathalie.vanreeth@skynet.be

The children's rooms and the bathrooms each have their own colour accents, yet the same materials were selected: glass mosaic and stained Carrara marble. Vola faucets and wall light by Cubetto.

FUNCTIONAL YET WARM AND INTIMATE

This children's room was designed by Nathalie Van Reeth with furniture in stained oak.
The result is a functional yet warm and intimate room.

nathalie.vanreeth@skynet.be

Plaid and pillows by Missoni.

PICTURESQUE

A picturesque coastside villa was thoroughly restored.
The outer volume and the appearance of the residence had to remain identical
so as to not disturb the existing coast style and the image of the village.
The clients asked Nathalie Van Reeth to design a true family home.
The volumes were reconsidered, the attic was utilised and the
basements were dug out to create extra storage space. The limited number of
materials and the monochrome colour pallet create a sober, taut whole.

nathalie.vanreeth@skynet.be

The children's rooms are located in the attic space. The roof framing is finished in roughly planed, white painted boards. Boarded floor in aged oak. Furniture in varnished mdf.

DIFFERENT ACCENTS

These children's rooms, another design by Nathalie Van Reeth, have
been created with custom made furniture in varnished mdf, yet with
Missoni accents for the girls and Libeco grey linen for the boys.

nathalie.vanreeth@skynet.be

A HOLIDAY HOME NEAR THE BEACH

Nathalie Van Reeth transformed a former hotel from 1960, situated on a long
stretch of white, sand beach into a modern holiday home for a young family.

nathalie.vanreeth@skynet.be

The bathroom floor is tiled with white zelliges. Washbasin finished in white tadelakt.

Brisk, playful colours in the children's room. Vintage furniture and a Turkish kilim.

A TRUE HOLIDAY FEEL

These children's rooms have been created by Ensemble & Associés in a Mi Casa house.
When you enter this home, you are overwhelmed by a true holiday feel.

www.ensembleetassocies.be

The children's bathroom is finished in lacquered medium.

SURROUNDED BY NATURE

This small village home was completely transformed to house a young family.
The resolutely contemporary interior, in contrast with the authentic
character of the facades, was rethought to maximise the space.
A house where it is pleasant to spend time, surrounded by beautiful nature.

www.ensembleetassocies.be

The children's bathroom in beveka. Taps by Dornbracht.

YOUNG AND CONTEMPORARY

A young, modern bedroom in a contemporary country house.
A design by XVL Projects (Xavier Van Lil).

www.xvl.eu

PARADISE IN PINK

This villa, typical of Normandy, has been renovated by architect Christine von der Becke and interior designer Nathalie Van Reeth. The daughter's room and bathroom are a real paradise in pink: pink zelliges in the bathroom and shades of pastel pink in the bedroom.

nathalie.vanreeth@skynet.be   www.christinevonderbecke.be

ANNO 1642

This house, dating back to 1642, with its four bays and saddleback roof in the traditional brick and sandstone style and its abutting nineteenth-century buildings, has been restored and radically re-modelled by architect Bernard De Clerck to make it a fully fledged contemporary home for a family with three young children. The owners wished to put all the rooms to their best use, enjoying the magnificent surroundings and making use of the natural light, orientation and straightforward materials such as stone, wood and whitewash. This is a house that radiates peace and simplicity, in perfect harmony with the untouched landscape with its old orchard.

info@bernarddeclerck.be

The bedrooms of the three daughters.

THE CONTEMPORARY RENOVATION
OF A FORMER HUNTING LODGE

In the green countryside outside Bruges, in the middle of a 150-hectare nature reserve,
interior architect Ann Gryp has renovated this former hunting lodge as her own home.
The transformation of the country house was a radical one: almost everything was altered.
The final result is sober and contemporary with a warm touch.

The boys' room with its dressing room and bathroom is also accessible via a separate staircase.
The white-painted planks underline the youthful character of this room.

The shower in the children's bathroom has been clad with river stones, as has the relaxation space in the basement.

A BLEND OF TIMELESS AND CONTEMPORARY:
A BALANCED PHILOSOPHY FOR LIVING

This farmhouse was created by architect Stéphane Boens. The owners also use
the house as a showroom for am projects, their interior-design company.
Their work is more a philosophy of life than simply decoration.
They create timeless environments and living spaces that are perfectly in balance
with the lifestyle of their clients. They decorated this house themselves.

www.stephaneboens.be   www.amprojects.be

Custom-made boxspring beds for both boy's rooms.

THE COMPLETE TRANSFORMATION
OF A BELLE EPOQUE COUNTRY HOUSE

A Belle Epoque country house, built between 1890 and 1920, was
gently renovated by the owners, a family with three children.
The existing pine floor has been retained for the children's rooms
and restored in all of their rooms and in the bathrooms.
A long space under the roof leads to the music studio.

LIVING IN A RESTORED FARMHOUSE

This 19th-century farmhouse with a courtyard has been
freshened up and given a more contemporary feel.
Original elements were retained as far as possible, and nothing
about the existing structure of the house was changed: a respectful renovation.

The eldest daughter's bedroom and adjoining study. Bed by Treca de Paris, elm bedside table by am projects with a lamp by Catherine Memmi.

The children's bathroom with white-painted washstand with a Carrara marble surface.

↖
The youngest daughter's room, also with a bed by Treca and a canopy with fabric by Ralph Lauren.

A ROMANTIC GIRL'S ROOM

This renovation project was entrusted to Sphere Concepts. They contacted architect Gerd Van Zundert (AID-Architects) to adapt the outer walls and to bring these into the correct proportions, after Sphere Concepts had designed the interior layout. The previous layout of the villa was dated, and Sphere Concepts replaced this with an interior that radiates charm, and in particular peace and quiet. Axes and through-views were incorporated where possible, the right materials were chosen, and all colours and finishing trims were decided on with a view to achieving a harmonious and balanced end result.

www.sphereconcepts.be

The children's bathroom has been fitted out entirely symmetrically. A Boffi shower cubicle and taps that change colour make for a special atmosphere.

COSY MINIMALISM

Interior designer Dries Dols was faced with a major challenge when he took on this project. He had to create a timeless contemporary interior in a conventional residence with a lot of traditional elements. And what's more, all the members of the family had their own very specific (and differing) views on what makes a successful living environment. For Dries Dols it was an enthralling assignment, and one in which he has succeeded wonderfully well. Every member of the family has been made to feel completely at home here. The end result looks particularly restful, minimalist and yet cosy.

www.dols.nl   www.elfcreators.com

The nursery, with its traditional cupboards and taut lines, provides a good basis for development into a children's room.

The floor in the children's bathroom is laid in polished concrete. Bathroom cupboards in solid oak and a washbasin in composite stone. The shower is finished off with white painted glass.

PEACE AND QUIET

Costermans Villa Projects built a timeless country house adjacent
to a natural pond and surrounded by lovely trees. The atmosphere
in the residence is airy and warm, and shirks excess.
The overall concept radiates peace and quiet and reliability, and
the right combinations of materials and meticulously designed
custom-made items provide for an intimist, cosy ambience.

www.costermans-projecten.be

In this children's room lively colours were used, the gradated blue Moroccan zelliges tiles blending beautifully with the grey natural stone.

A LAKESIDE RESIDENCE NEAR GENEVA

This summer house on Lake Geneva used to be part of the «Domaine de Chanivaz». It was bought by a young family and fully renovated by Sphere Concepts. Located on a spit of land between Geneva and Laussane in the Vaud, this estate has a fabulous view over the French side of Lake Leman where you can admire the snow-capped mountains even in summer. The listed outer walls were conserved, but inside the residence all dividing walls and mezzanine floors were taken out, and raised where possible. The residence was given a completely new floor plan and fitted out with an extra room as a guest accommodation unit built into the mountain. The microclimate means that living in «Les Fontanettes» is simply marvellous.

www.sphereconcepts.be

Every children's room has
a 160cm-wide Nilson bed,
shower unit and cockpit desk.

↖
The low attic with a
Roche Bobois sitting area,
a cushioned three-piece
suite with adjustable
back in vivid colours.

ANGLO-SAXON INSPIRATION

Ilse De Meulemeester created this residence in close cooperation with villa builder Elbeko and the architects' firm of engineer and architect Bart François. The assignment seemed simple: to design a timeless country house with the historical impact of a traditional English cottage, which would be a beacon of peace and quiet and a place with a permanent holiday feel to it.

www.bartfrancois.be   www.ilsedemeulemeester.be

A CHIC HOME IN A CLASSIC GEORGIAN RESIDENCE

The interior of this classic Georgian residence in North London was recently completed by the design team Laxer + Salter. The designers, who specialise in contemporary classic interior furnishings and fittings, created a chic living environment that is elegant yet at the same time practical and convenient in terms of everyday living. The occupants are a young family. This residence is typical of Laxer + Salter's trademark style: a mixture of luxury, polished design and comfortable living. Laxer + Salter's cooperation is based on a shared aim to create exclusive, top-of-the-range interiors throughout Europe and the U.S.A. Their philosophy consists in combining the client's idea with local aesthetics in order to create a bespoke and genuinely individual residence. For this project the design team worked with F3 Architects in London, a firm of architects and interior designers that designs timeless and artistic interiors.

www.rlaxerinteriors.com   www.f3architects.co.uk

The children's rooms.
Eclectic mirror and art are mixed with white simple furnishings and easily changeable fabrics are designed to suit the evolving needs of growing children. These joyful rooms are both childlike but well suited to the entire feeling of the overall home.

HOLIDAY FEELING IN GSTAAD

This chalet, near the exclusive, traffic-free Swiss village of Gstaad, was designed by the local architects Tschanz Architektur AG. The new owners – a couple with three adult children – bought the whole chalet, which was originally divided into three apartments. They contacted Sphere Concepts and asked them to come up with a complete design for their holiday home. As the chalet is also used in the summer months, Sphere opted for a lighter, contemporary look that contrasts with the solid, rustic interior of traditional chalets.

www.sphereconcepts.be

The children's bedrooms have a real holiday atmosphere. Bedding by Scapa and Donaldson.
The bunk beds were custom-made. Curtains and blinds by Designers Guild and Romo.

THE CHILDREN'S ROOMS
OF TWO MOUNTAIN CHALETS

At a client's request, Marina Wenger (Version M) designed and built two apartments in the mountains. The entire residence radiates a contemporary yet warm and intimate feel, with timeless materials and objects.

www.versionm.com

The convivial children's room with four bunk beds, inspired by the sleeping-places in mountain refuges.

Another children's room designed by Marina Wenger (Version M) with four bunk beds. There is storage space under the beds.

In this children's room provision is made for four bunk beds. The paintings of bears were made to order.

AN ORANGE AND WHITE COLOUR EXPLOSION

This children's room and bathroom is situated in a residential project with four ultramodern lofts transformed by Upptown, with Bruno Corbisier as architect. The streamlined, minimalist design gives way to an orange/white colour explosion. There could hardly be a stronger contrast with the black/white accents in the rest of the house.

The children's bathroom has a different atmosphere, with a harmonious colour palette in white and pale green.

TWO CHILDREN'S ROOMS IN LONDON

This stately residence in London's Holland Park was built in 1862 by the architects William & Francis Radford. Winny Vangroenweghe, architect with Obumex, created and coordinated the complete renovation and layout of the premises into a timeless and harmonious whole, where the hectic character of the metropolis is quickly forgotten…

www.obumex.be

The children's rooms.
Bunk bed and table in the boys' room are by DucDuc (NY).
The small table and the tree in one of the girls' rooms are by Couverture in London.

COSY AND INTIMATE

The design of this low energy home, created by the architect Annik Dierckx, is timeless and practical. The newest materials and most recent technologies were used. The children's rooms are cosy and intimate.

www.adarchitectuur.be

THE BRIGHT CHILDREN'S ROOMS OF CASA NERO

Casa Nero refers to the name of the interior design agency of the owners (Casa Vero) and
to the black brick volume that makes up their home, designed by BBSC-Architects.
The children's rooms are not black, though: both children sleep among bright colours.

www.casavero.be

LOFT STORY

This 500 m² loft in the heart of London is one of the favourite recent projects of interior designer Raoul Cavadias. The bare area only consisted of several technical columns and a single wall with twelve windows on the north side. The owners had an extensive list of demands: they wanted to retain the look of the original depots, there had to be three bedrooms each with a bathroom and dressing room, an open kitchen, a laundry, salon, office, fireplace, library, a lot of storage space... and a large aquarium. Above all they wanted lots of space.

www.raoul-cavadias.com

View of the bathroom with a luminous bath by Aquamass. The wash basin with the mirror was designed by Starck.

↖
The girl's room with transparent walls, like a spaceship.
Chair made of methacrylate Rainbow by Patrick Norguet.

COSMOPOLITAN FEELING

This complete structure was designed by interior architect Nathalie Deboel in collaboration with Obumex. In consultation with the client Obumex chose for the ground floor: a fully customised and personalised interior, where the client can find complete peace and harmony. The consistent use of dark tinted Spanish oak and bronze gives the interior a warm atmosphere. This allows the contemporary artworks to come perfectly into their own. The combination of a timeless and elegant interior with art and antique results in a cosmopolitan whole.

www.obumex.be   www.nathaliedeboel.be

The children's bedroom with chairs by Poul Kjaerholm. The striped wall was inspired by the work of Daniel Buren.

BABY & CO:
A PARADISE FOR (FUTURE) PARENTS

Baby & Co is a specialist store for nurseries and new babies' wish lists,
established in a stately mansion on the Quellinstraat in Antwerp.
Within 600 m² quality conscious (future) parents will find all the top brands for their
baby: Théophile & Patachou, Caramella, Woodwork, Tartine & Chocolat, Martinelli,
Stokke, Bugaboo, Peg perego, Mountain Buggy, Maxi-Cosi, Hilfiger and many others.
They can allow themselves to be inspired by one of the fourteen beautifully arranged
baby and junior rooms with matching decorations in the showroom of Baby & Co.
Baby & Co has its own installation service and after sale service.

www.babyenco.be
0032/(0)3/226.35.62

The "Baldaquin" room from Théophile & Patachou, with bedding and accessories from their "Denim" collection.

The "Antique" room from Théophile & Patachou, with "Flocon" accessories and bedding.

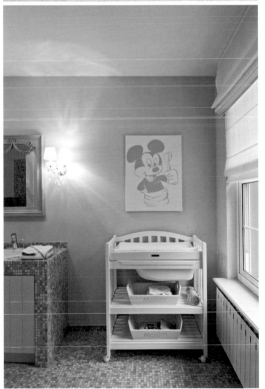

The «Antique» room from
Théophile & Patachou with
«Poudre» bedding and accessories,
also from Théophile & Patachou.

A cradle from Théophile
& Patachou.

The room «Will» from Woodwork with «Flanelle» from Théophile & Patachou.

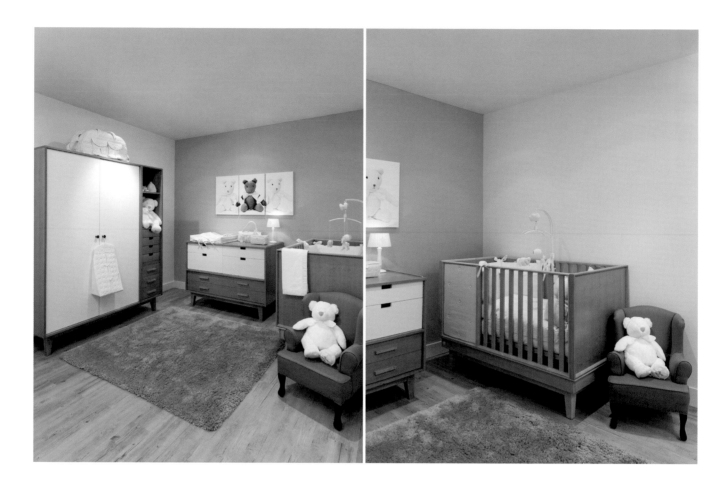

The «Fifty» room from Théophile & Patachou with «Nuage», also from Théophile & Patachou.

A PERFECT BALANCE BETWEEN CLASSIC AND MODERN

Benedikte Lecot is an interior designer who aims to create a symbiosis of functionality, atmosphere, light and architecture in all of her projects. She aims to achieve a unity of style within a pleasant living environment that balances classic and modern, and which is always in keeping with the individual needs and desires of the client. All of her designs are therefore created à la carte. The exclusive character of her interiors is further reinforced by perfect workmanship, carried out by experienced and passionate professionals.

www.b-lecot.be

The boys' bedroom. An extra-long desk with a view of the garden.

↖
Shades of white and pink in
this girls' bedroom.

PLAYFUL DETAILS

In this report, project developer Alexander Cambron and interior architect Fabienne Dupont present two children's rooms with playful details in one of their recent creations. A few touches of bright colour, with the rest painted white.

www.alexandershouses.com   www.fabathome.be

Two children's rooms and bathrooms with playful details: heart-shaped mirrors, an illuminated bath and wall, and pebble tiles. A few touches of bright colour, with the rest painted white.

COSY HOME IN SOLID WOOD

Mi Casa does not only wish to construct houses that are safe, functional, durable and comfortable. The company also strives to create beautiful, personalised homes, in which the architecture and decoration reflect the philosophy and wishes of the owners. The wood of the Nordic red pine exhibits more natural warmth and charm than the wood of local trees.

www.micasa.be

Their natural appearance means that wooden walls require little decoration. The owner immediately feels at home because the walls do not seem bare and unfinished or cause the room to echo unpleasantly.

PERFECT HARMONY

This room has been created by interior architect Tina Boumans in a house inspired by the prairie houses of Frank Lloyd Wright with an austere but warm character. The child's room has a made-to-measure desk and dressing table. The wall behind the bed is separated from the ceiling, so that the room seems to extend.

tina.b@telenet.be

A WARM AND CONTEMPORARY RECTORY-STYLE HOUSE

In this report, interior architect Tina Boumans showcases two more children's rooms.
The cupboards in the children's rooms are grooved: a strong wink by the designer towards
the rustic character of the house. These rooms were painted with a brush to introduce
structure. The tailor-made design fills up the room nicely and there are no lost spaces.

tina.b@telenet.be

WARM FEEL IN AN AUSTERE DESIGN

In spite of the austere design from architect's office PVL Popeye - Van Landschoot, this is a house that radiates atmosphere and warmth. This is achieved by the material use, and by not hiding everything in the interior behind fair-faced cupboard doors. The dark tinted oak floors and cupboard walls, the velvet curtains and the warm, light colours bring cheerfulness and joy into this house, including the teenager's rooms and play area.

www.pvlarchitecten.be

CONTEMPORARY AND TIMELESS

RR Interior Concepts propagates a lifestyle philosophy which is contemporary, but also timeless. Strong brands by well-known designers, furniture that never dates, interiors in which it is pleasant to live. The two children's rooms in this report illustrate this philosophy.

www.rrinterieur.be

STREAMLINED, CLASSIC AND CHIC

Chris van Eldik and Wendy Jansen opened an interior-design company about ten years ago in Wijk bij Duurstede in the Netherlands, called De Zon van Duurstede (The Sun of Duurstede). Their style can best be described as "streamlined classic": a combination of warm, natural, honest, basic materials and fabrics, but in a definitely contemporary, almost minimalist setting. This husband-and-wife team were among the pioneers of lime paints, which have enjoyed great success in recent years. The choice of these paints is completely in keeping with their designs, which are timeless, sober and cosy, all at the same time. Chris and Wendy also design their own furniture line under the name of JOB interiors. They started with chairs and sofas, and then went on to create a collection of refectory tables.

www.jobinterieur.nl

The bedroom of daughter Ijf is in pink lime paint.

THE CHILDREN'S ROOMS OF A HISTORIC NOTARY'S HOUSE

This notary's house dates from 1807. The main building has all the charm of a grand, historic home. The extensions, designed by Stéphane Boens, have a more country feel and are completely integrated into their surroundings. Authenticity and simplicity were the most important principles in this project. White was therefore an obvious choice as the basic colour, as it emphasises the pure and beautiful character of the space. Colour was introduced through the furniture and objects, which also reinforce the pure and sober appearance: a kind of minimalism, but with old materials. All of the paintwork is by Frank Verschuere; most of the furniture is from am projects. Both of the children's rooms are in the attic. The walls and beams in the bedroom of son César are finished in white lime paint. This old bed has been painted in different layers of lime paint (blue/green) to create an antiquated effect.

www.amprojects.be   frankverschuere@bvbafrankverschuere.be

MARITIME FEEL

Project Broersbankhelling, which is named after the sandbank in the sea close to this street,
is the work of the firm of architects Popeye - Van Landschoot and architect Marc Corbiau.
The entire building is made of concrete and wood.
Concrete was used as the solid base for the two lowest layers of the construction,
with wood for the two upper layers with split-level apartments.
The floor and walls of the children's room are clad with wood.

www.pvlarchitecten.be

The use of pale-coloured pebble tiles in these bathrooms completes the seaside atmosphere.

LIGHT AND SPACE IN A SEASIDE APARTMENT

Two smaller seaside flats were converted by Virginie & Odile Dejaegere
to make one large apartment: a holiday home with a simple design that
corresponds perfectly to the needs of a young family with children.

dejaegere_interiors@hotmail.com

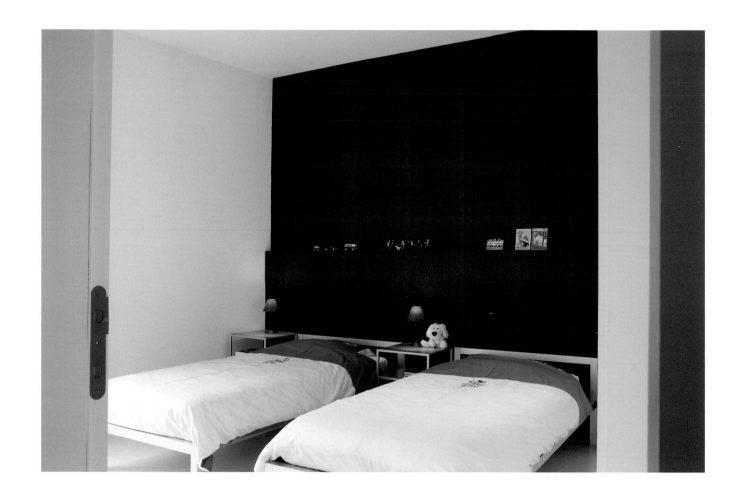

EXTRA DEPTH

This city apartment initially presented rather a lot of difficulties, including the number of small, dark rooms. Interior design ageny Pas-Partoe took on the challenge of transforming this neglected property into a light, spacious and modern home. In consultation with architect Karel Beeck (who supervised the structural work), an number of interior walls were demolished. All doors were designed to be ceiling height, including in the children's bedroom and bathroom. The dark colour in the bedroom adds extra depth.

www.pas-partoe.be

View of the children's room with its MDF-panel floor, laid in strips and finished with six layers of boat varnish. A walk-in shower. Taps by Boffi. The assymetry of the washstands, the spot illumination of the white bathroom furniture and the ceiling-height doors give emphasis to this compact space.

A REFUGE FOR THE CHILDREN

The Themenos architects and interior designers tend to feel a certain responsibility for the lifestyle of the people who live in their buildings. Bedrooms are a very important room in the house: they should be a refuge, including for the children.

www.themenos.be

Wood panelling has been installed in the children's room, ensuring a sense of warmth and safety.

LONG ISLAND STYLE

This teenager's bedroom in Long Island style has been designed by Francis Luypaert, with integrated LED and atmospheric lighting.

www.francisluypaert.be

HAPPY COLOURS

These children's rooms in bright. happy colours
are designed by RR Interior Concepts.

www.rrinterieur.be

BRIGHT GREEN AND PASTEL

This villa, built in around 1950, has been thoroughly restored by the Antwerp interior-architecture studio P&M Projects to make a contemporary classic living environment. A neat, discreet and timeless house with a child's room in bright green and pastel colours.

www.pm-projects.be

SENSE OF SPACE AND CALM

The interior of a stylish country house, created by Vlassak-Verhulst, has been
designed by Sphere Concepts in a contemporary and timeless ambience.
The children's rooms have the same sense of space and calm as the rest of the house.

www.sphereconcepts.be

The children's bathroom is clad with white Carrara marble.

A room in shades of blue with a Treca bed and Donaldson cushions.

ENDLESS VIEWS

Nothing remains of the original appearance of these four houses from the 1950s which were combined into a contemporary and luxurious single-family home. The restructuring of its various levels and functionality revolved around a patio which now lets natural light into the heart of the house. With taste and determination, the owner allowed Oliver and Hélène Lempereur to go to the end with their ideas, even for the three children's rooms...

www.olivierlempereur.com

A SUITE FOR THE DAUGHTER

This 1908 villa by the architect Jozef Viérin has been built in an eclectic style. The old property was empty and had been left desolate for years. The team from project developer Alexander Cambron and interior architect Fabienne Dupont realised a rigorous restoration, in which the existing charm of the home was preserved. The top floor was painted black and white for the daughter with a seating area in the tower.

www.alexandershouses.com   www.fabathome.be

A TRUE CHARMING HOME

This charming villa urgently needed renovation. The old stone drive with metre-high rhododendrons was preserved. The interior spaces were small however, so the kitchen was extended with a few rooms above it. The straw roof, extended and renewed, gives an extra cachet. The façade was finished with greige whitewash and black steel windows. The garden was evened with the patio, with for ancient beeches at the end. The swimming pool was renewed by the owner with black slate and a wooden deck around it. The original oak beams and doors gave a sombre impression and were given a white patina as a result. All the old elements were preserved and reworked, stained, updated,… to blow new life into the villa: that is precisely the charm of this home.

www.alexandershouses.com   www.fabathome.be

All the children's rooms were put under the eaves: pink for the baby, taupe for the son with a mezzanine for a dressing room and bathroom and the attic was furnished for the daughter, with silver-painted beams, pink details and lots of white. The bathroom was finished here with wooden floorboards.

A REAL FAMILY HOME

This existing, small villa was transformed into a living environment with a lot of space and a sea of light. The house was extended with a huge wooden orangery, the existing outside walls remained intact, with new window openings as a passage between the two living rooms. The renovation was realised according to the style of the house, rustic and yet with a modern touch. It is a real family home where everyone has their place, from young to old.

www.alexandershouses.com   www.fabathome.be

FULL OF CHARACTER

These children's rooms full of character were furnished by Pas-Partoe with a custom-designed desk. The high bed with bed skirt comes from the Orizzonti collection. The reading lamp is a design from the 1950s.

www.pas-partoe.be

A new solid oak floor was painted white in the children's bathrooms. The shower and basin are fitted with Vola taps.

The attic was fully insulated and renovated. The carpeting is 100% sisal.

SPACE AND LIGHT
IN A CONTEMPORARY COUNTRY HOUSE

This stately mansion was designed by architect Philippe Mortelmans at the behest of a
family with three young children. The interior is a creation of Annick Grimmelprez.
The house is idyllically situated in Schilde, a green suburb close to Antwerp.
Each room offers a view of the protected forest area and this house is perfectly
matched to the wishes of the owners: contemporary, with a strong feeling of light and
space, where precious materials have been used and a few colourful highlights.
The result: a cosy home in an oasis of tranquillity and wellness.

info@annickgrimmelprez.be

The daughter's bedroom, with an oak floor and white
painted dressing room wall.
Purple-violet-coloured curtains and a desk with separate
drawers in white lacquer ware, night lamp in shiny
chrome and a bed reading lamp by JNL.

Contrasts of white walls with dark windows and dark, red-lined blinds for the boy's room.
A door that slides completely into the wall connects the room to the bathroom.

The boy's bathroom with an arched doorway into the shower and toilet. The floor is in dark brown marble mosaic, bath and washbasin surrounds in Silestone Bianco Zeus. Stools by Christian Liaigre.

THE ATTRACTIONS OF AN ANCIENT FARMHOUSE

The Heerlijkheid van Marrem is a genuine farmhouse whose
oldest remnants date from the seventeenth century.
The «poorthuys» (gatehouse), the stable wing, the «graenschuur» (granary) and the
walls have all been given heritage status by the Department of Monuments.
The farm was in a terrible condition when the current owners bought it three years ago.
In consultation with an enthusiastic builder and site supervisor, and without using an
architect, they turned the semi-ruin into a charming home with all modern comforts.

www.heerlijkheidvanmarrem.be   www.amprojects.be   www.obumex.be   www.dirkcousaert.be

The hall on the upper floor now connects the upper and lower spaces: previously the building consisted after all of the farmer's manor house and the building below for the workers.
Stairs by Dirk Cousaert; all cabinets and wardrobes were made by Obumex.

The attic space with its original roof trusses was transformed into a small apartment for the eldest son.

INSPIRED BY THE ENGLISH COUNTRYSIDE

Home Development Company built this English inspired
villa in the green belt around Antwerp.
Warm, natural materials were chosen for the exterior,
perfectly in harmony with the green surroundings.

www.homedc.be

The children's beds were completely custom made. The floor is covered with French oak parquet. The children had a say in the furnishing of their bedrooms. The daughter can enjoy a fine view over the garden from her desk.

The boy's room has a more masculine finish. The three windows allow a nice entry of light and a fine view over the garden. A cupboard wall in grooved MDF.

A PASSION FOR BEAUTY

In this project, the architect Stéphane Boens deals in a masterly way with
the rich architectural heritage adding a very personal touch to it.
In close consultation with the owners, Boens created a unique home where tradition and artisanal
techniques, modern comfort and a passion for beauty merge into a uniquely harmonious whole.

www.stephaneboens.be   www.obumex.be

The daughter's bedroom with a bed from Anker Bedding and Tai Ping carpet in ecru. An "Amande" lamp from Liaigre in bronze was given a white patina.

A PASSION FOR WOOD

These children's rooms and play area have been created in a solid wood construction by Mi Casa.

www.micasa.be

PARADISE FOR A LITTLE PRINCESS

This apartment is part of a residential development in
Nankang, Taipei designed by Mark Lintott.
The interior space covers approximately 350 m².
The development is primarily aimed at buyers from the nearby
high tech centre in Nankang Science Park.
As such, the apartment was designed to offer classic comfort updated
with the use of new materials and various high tech installations.

www.mld.tw

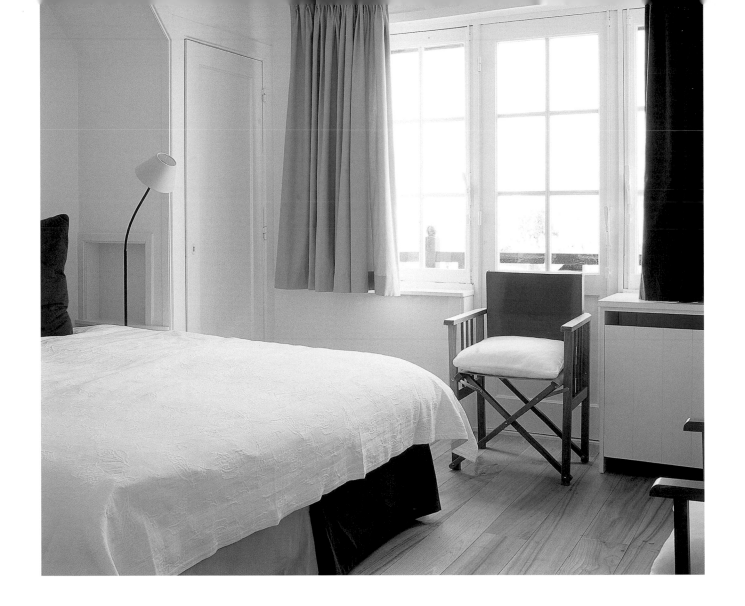

POETRY IN COLOURS

In this report, interior designer Dominique Koch (Zoute Nostalgie)
showcases two children's rooms in a seaside house.

CASTLE LIVING

A few years ago Anna and Andrew Barwick bought the 14th-century Château Rigaud, nestling
in the Gironde region near the historic town of St-Emilion and Bordeaux's top notch vineyards.
The castle was falling into disrepair, but the couple restored it completely and refurbished
it, complementing original features with distinguished, yet informal contemporary touches.
The new owners live with their two children in a converted outbuilding in the grounds of
the castle, while the vast 17th-century Chateau is rented out as a relaxing holiday location,
complete with a kitchen, a living room, nine en-suite bedrooms and a home cinema.
This report shows the children's nursery in the castle.

www.chateaurigaud.co.uk

AT HOME

Costermans Villa Projects designed and developed this timeless villa on
a beautiful site for a young family. The interior is modern and timeless,
suited to a family where growing children really feel at home.
Both the girls room (pages 216 to 219) and the boys room (pages 220-
221) have access to the second floor, with a hobby and play space.

www.costermans-projecten.be

219

AN ATTRACTIVE STYLE

A mansion with handsome Dutch gables, flanked by several outbuildings once more defines the view of the sun-drenched fields, with on the horizon the church steeple. Old materials, such as baked silver-coloured slate, natural stone,... were used in this important renovation by architect Bernard De Clerck. Details and ornamentation referring to the seventeenth and eighteenth century were used to return the whole complex to its original attractive style.

info@bernarddeclerck.be

The children's rooms have been painted in pale colours, with the addition of the favourite colour of each of the little daughters.

LONG ISLAND INSPIRATION

Architect Bart François was inspired for this design by Palladio's classicist villas: here the proportions can be found again of the classical Greek buildings which served as a base for the symmetrically constructed plans. His clients (a young, dynamic couple with two children) had a pronounced preference for the Long Island style... In any case it had to be a 'white' house: fresh, light ... hence the name WHIITE (with two I's), which turns up everywhere in the house (for instance on cushions, and on bedroom and bathroom textiles). The interior is a creation by Ilse De Meulemeester, in close consultation with the owners. In the children's rooms (with Boxspring beds) brushed oak planks were selected.

www.bartfrancois.be   www.ilsedemeulemeester.be

The floors in the bathrooms are clad with white Carrara marble (sandblasted). Tablets in polished
Carrara marble. All natural stone and tiles were supplied and placed by Dominique Desimpel. Bathroom design Van Marcke.

A COLOURFUL PARADISE

Interior design agency Van Staeyen created these
colourful children's rooms in a beautiful villa.

www.vanstaeyen.be

PUBLISHER
BETA-PLUS publishing
www.betaplus.com

PHOTOGRAPHY
Jo Pauwels

DESIGN
Polydem – Nathalie Binart

ISBN 13: 978-90-8944-116-4

Coordination production printing and binding :
www.belvedere.nl - André Kloppenberg
Printing and binding: Printer Trento, Italy